BIG MACHINES

written by Chris Oxlade
illustrated by Julian Baker

Ladybird

Words in **bold** are explained
in the glossary.

A catalogue record for this book is available
from the British Library

Published by Ladybird Books Ltd Loughborough Leicestershire UK
Ladybird Books Ltd is a subsidiary of the Penguin Group of Companies

© LADYBIRD BOOKS LTD MCMXCVI

BIG MACHINES

Contents

Mobile Crane

A mobile crane is like a truck with a crane on top. This means that the crane can be driven from place to place. It has a long arm called a **boom** which can reach high into the air. At the end of the boom is a long cable with a hook for lifting heavy loads. The driver sits in the front cab to drive along the road and moves into the back cab to work the crane when the truck stops.

A mobile crane has large, chunky tyres for driving across rough ground.

Long legs stretch out from each side of the crane to stop it tipping over when it lifts a heavy load.

The driver works the crane by pulling and pushing levers in the back cab.

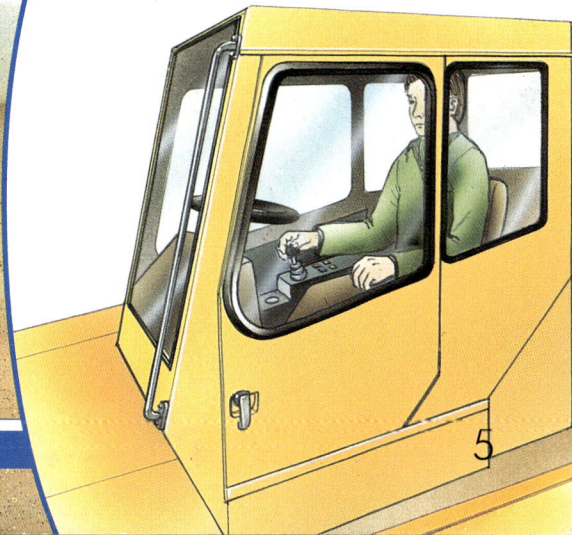

5

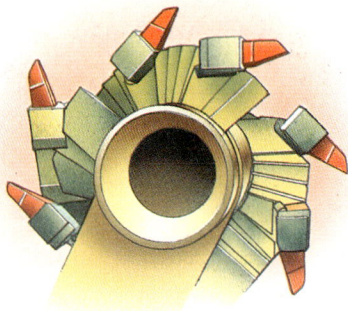

TBM's have large, sharp teeth which spin round and round, cutting into the rock.

Some of the engineers building the Channel Tunnel cycled to work and back.

One TBM dug from France and one from England. They met in the middle, deep under the sea.

Tunnel Boring Machine

You may never see a tunnel boring machine (or TBM for short) because it spends most of its time underground. The TBM in the picture is one of the machines which dug the Channel Tunnel under the sea between England and France. A machine like this burrows slowly along through the earth to make a tunnel. It removes all the **spoil** it makes and lines the new tunnel with concrete.

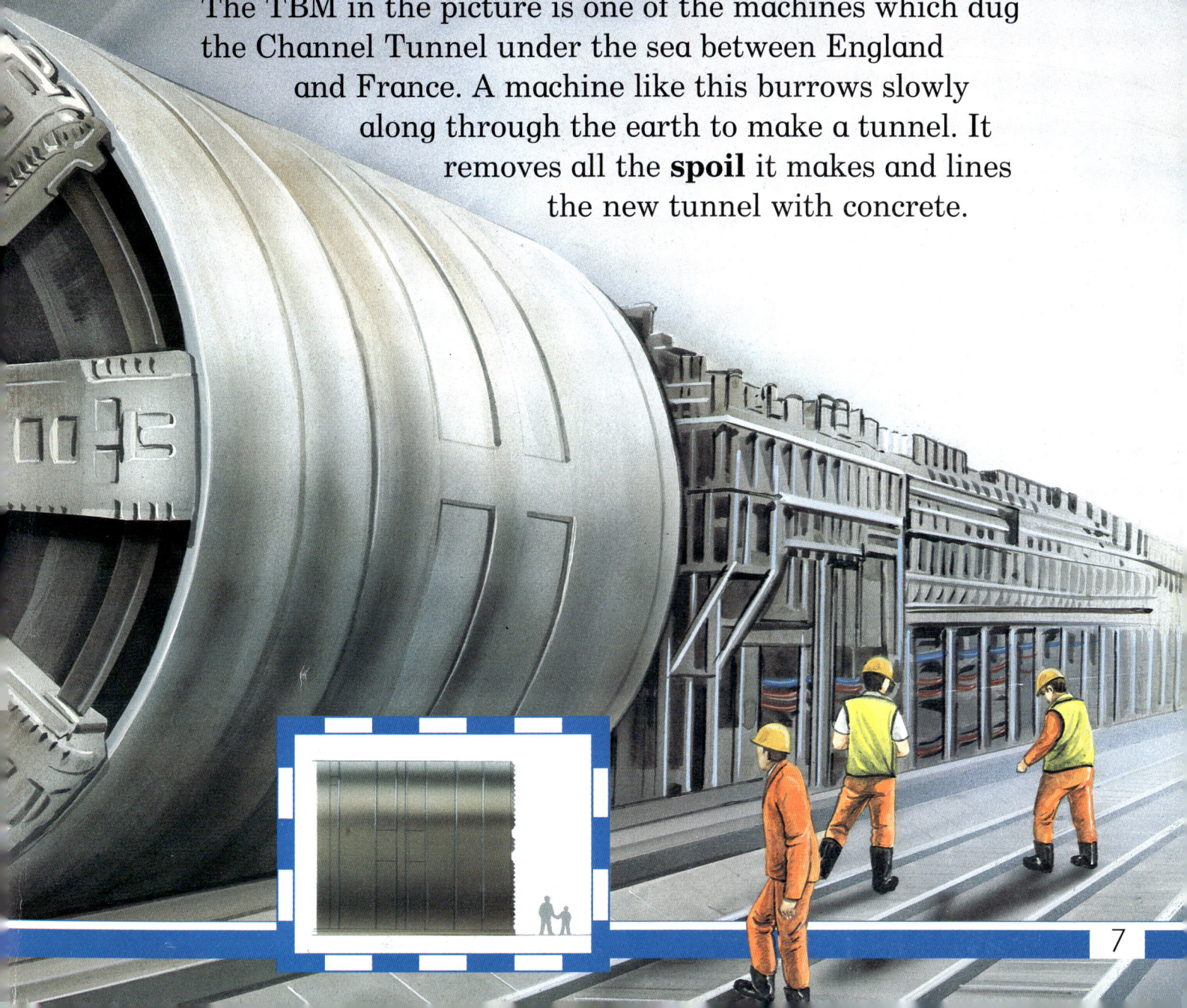

Car Crusher

A car crusher squashes old metal car bodies. The sides of the crusher begin to move in once the car body has been dropped into it. A lot of power is needed to squash the strong car body, so the crusher is worked by powerful **hydraulic pistons**. The car is squashed from all sides until it is just a small block. The blocks are then recycled. This means that the metal is used to make new cars.

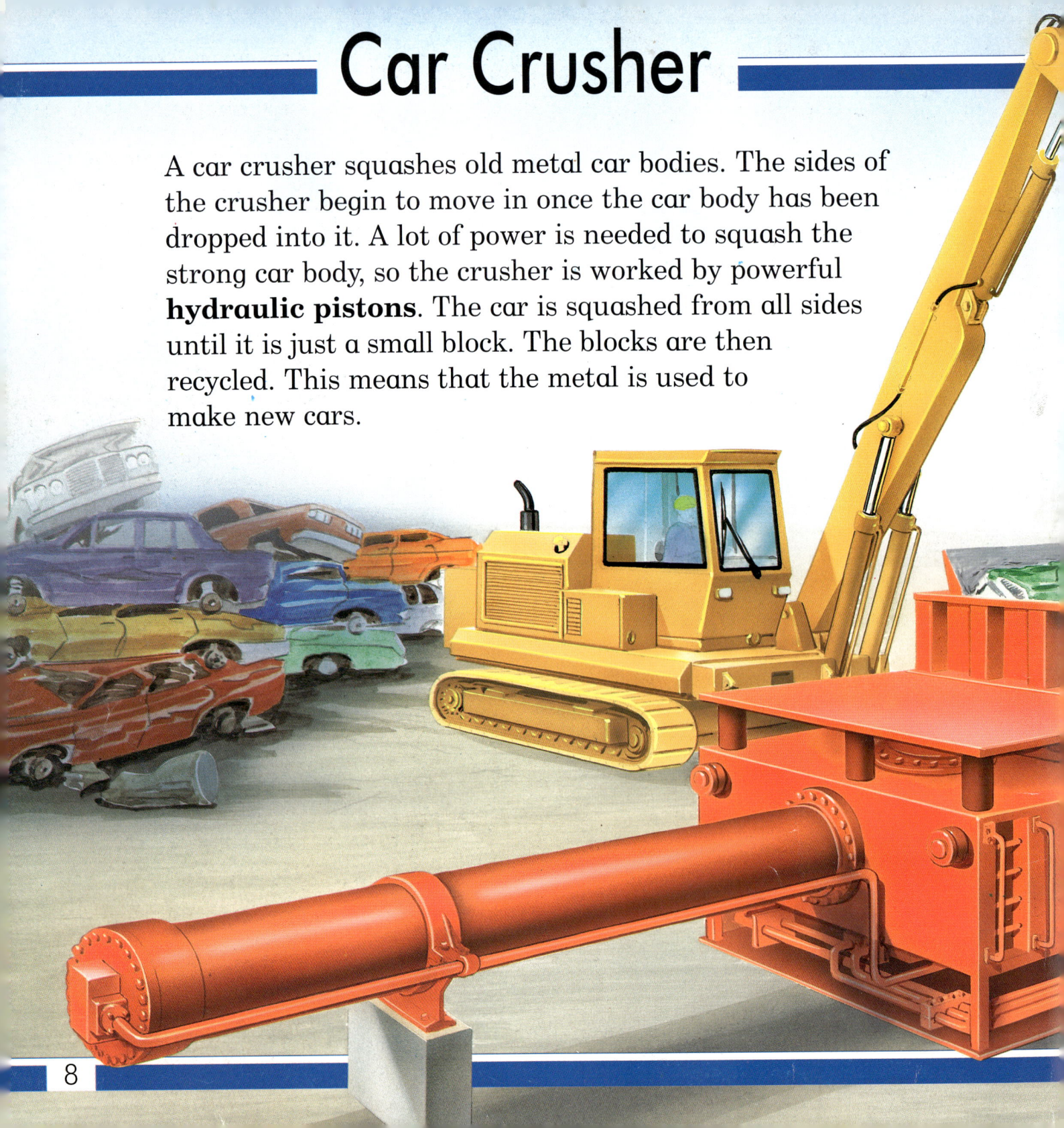

A tall crane picks up the wrecked cars with a huge mechanical grab. The driver opens the arms of the grab to drop the car into the crusher.

The crusher opens and the mechanical grab crane lifts out the block of metal.

Small pieces of metal are picked up by a huge electro-magnet.

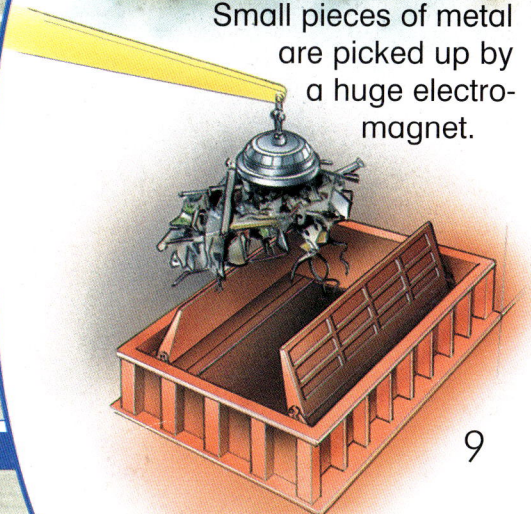

9

Tree Processor

A tree processor is a special machine used by forestry companies. It is used to cut tree trunks into planks of wood. It is powered by a **diesel engine** and has eight wide tyres. At the front it has a long 'arm' for picking up the tree trunks, which is worked by hydraulic pistons.

The tree processor grabs a tree in its long arm and cuts its trunk.

A special tool at the end of the arm strips off all the branches.

Another part of the machine cuts the stripped trunks into planks.

Wind Turbine

A wind turbine uses the power of the wind to make electricity. The wind makes the turbine blades spin round. This turns a **generator** which makes electricity. The stronger the wind blows, the more electricity can be produced. This picture shows three different sorts of wind turbine. They are built in places where it is usually very windy, such as on hill tops.

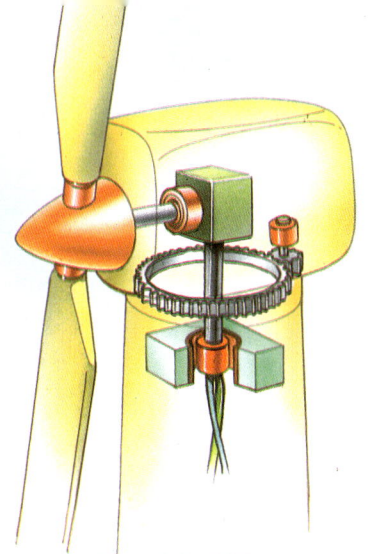

A motor turns the turbine round to make the blades point into the wind.

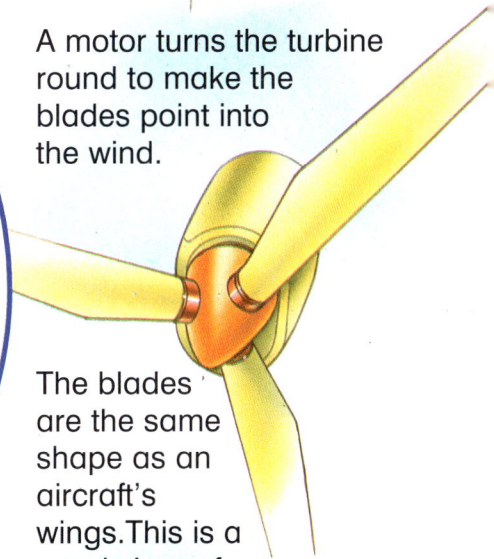

The blades are the same shape as an aircraft's wings. This is a good shape for catching the wind.

A large collection of wind turbines is known as a wind farm.

Robot Arm

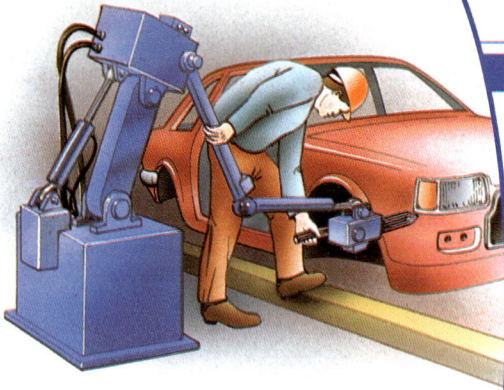

A human operator 'teaches' the robot arm all the moves it must make.

The robot arm repeats the moves exactly as it has been taught.

The hand-like tool at the end of the arm can be changed if the arm has to do a different job.

A robot arm can do all sorts of jobs. The arm in this picture is used in a car factory. It **welds** the metal parts of the car's body together. The robot arm is controlled by a computer which 'tells' it how to move. The arm is very strong and can easily lift the heavy welding tool. It can also move the tool about very accurately. And it never gets tired!

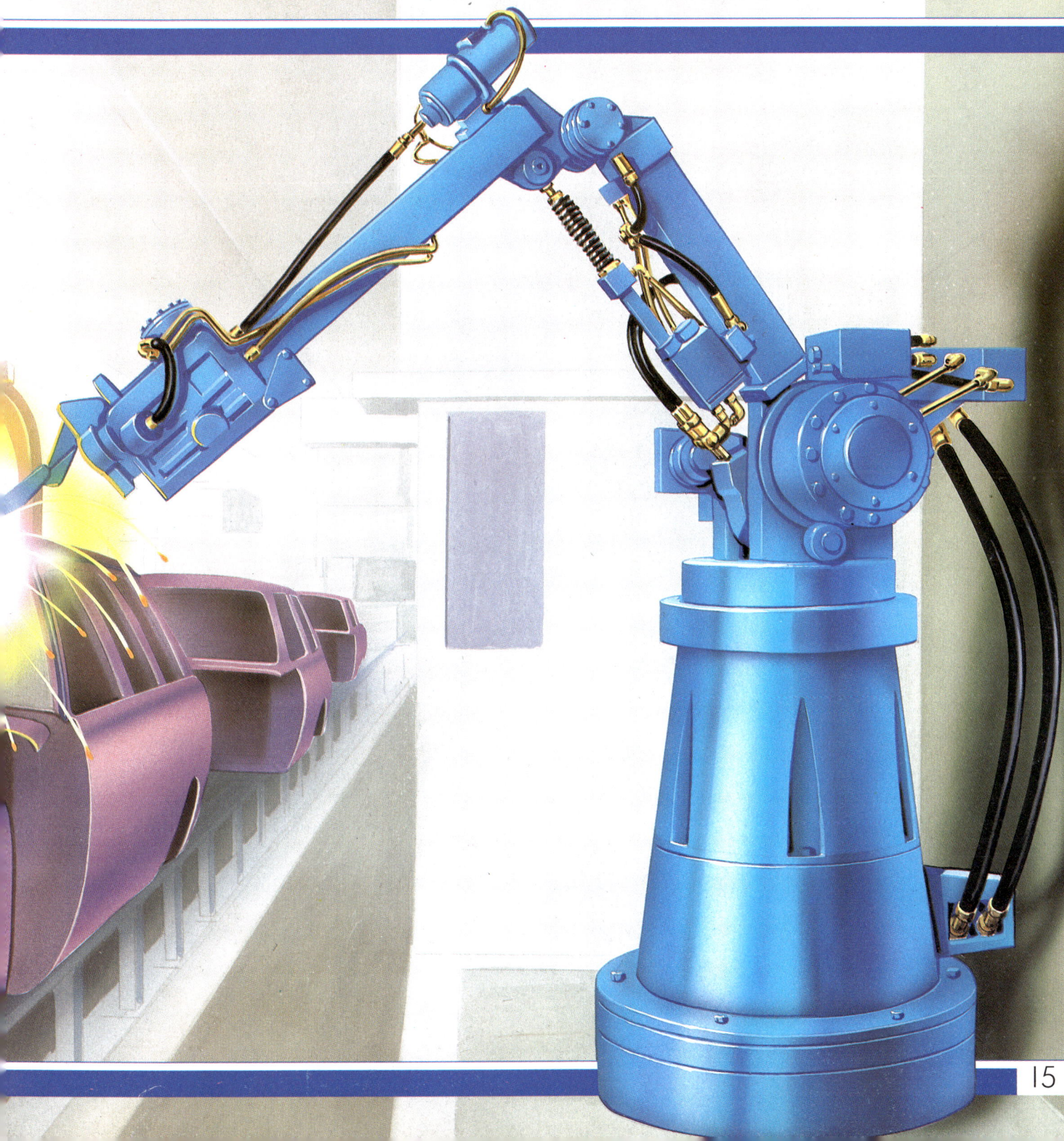

Rocket

A rocket is a flying machine which carries people and objects from the Earth into space. Most of the rocket is made up of huge fuel tanks. The fuel burns inside the engine, pushing the rocket upwards at high speed. The rocket shown here is called *Ariane*. It is launching a **satellite** into **orbit** high above the Earth.

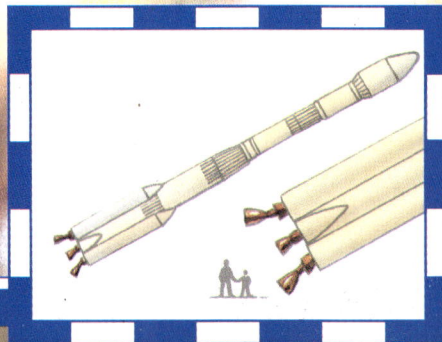

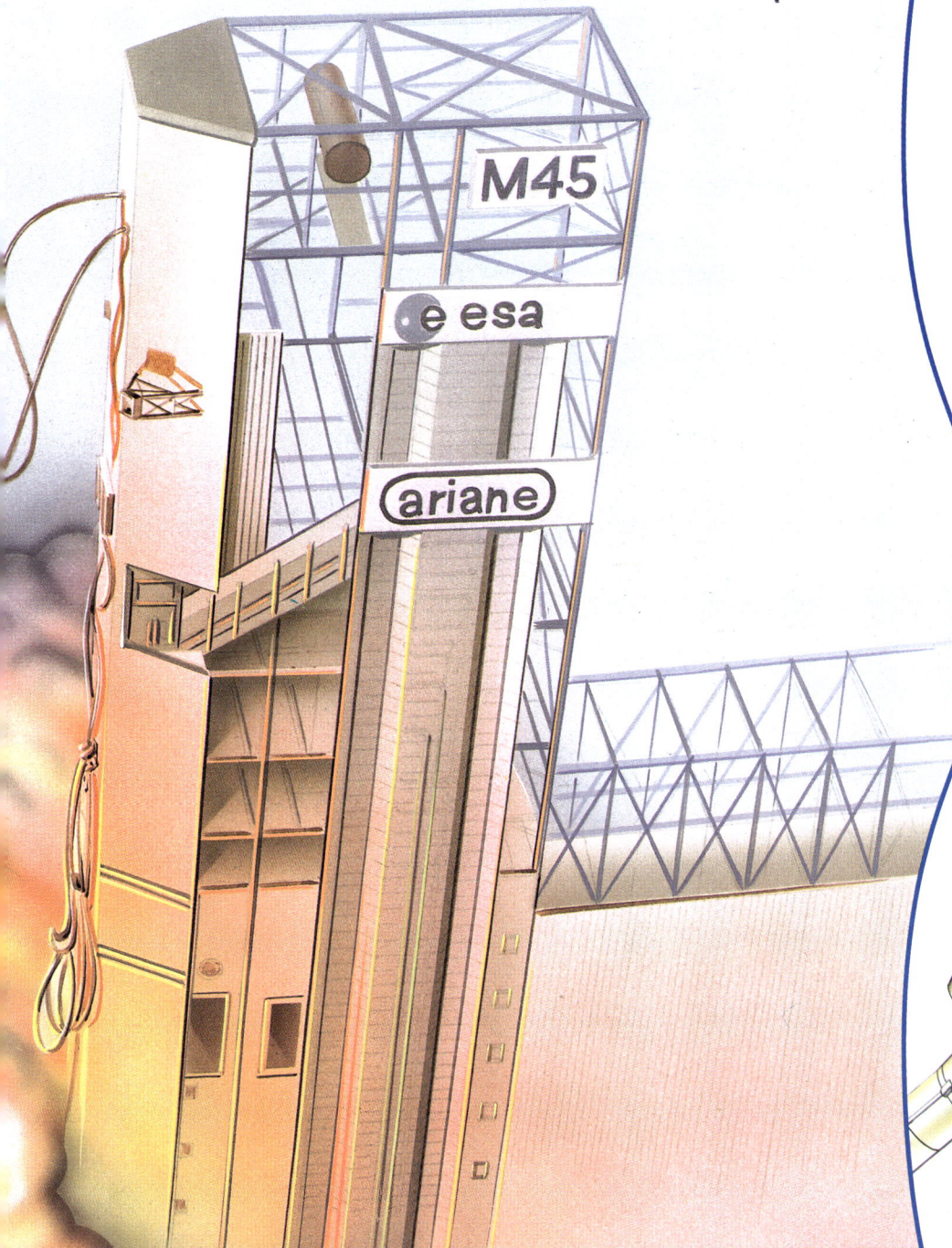

The rocket blasts off from its launch pad, powered by its first stage engine.

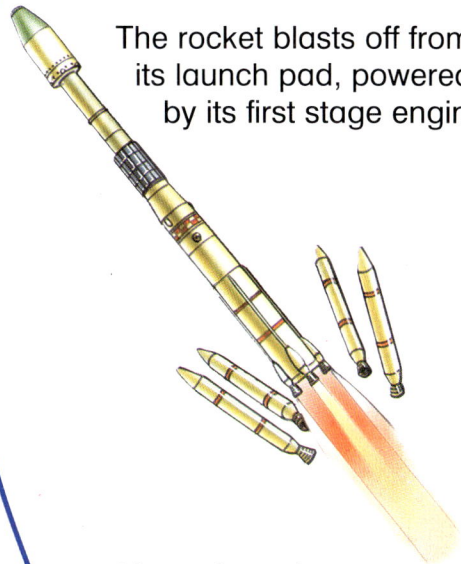

After a few minutes, the second stage engine takes over.

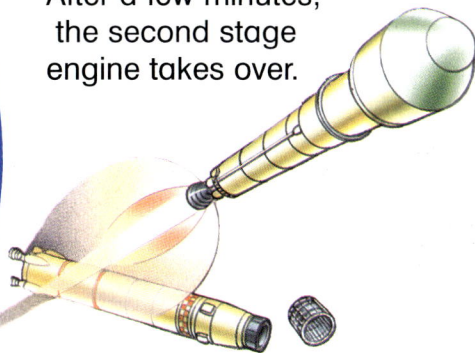

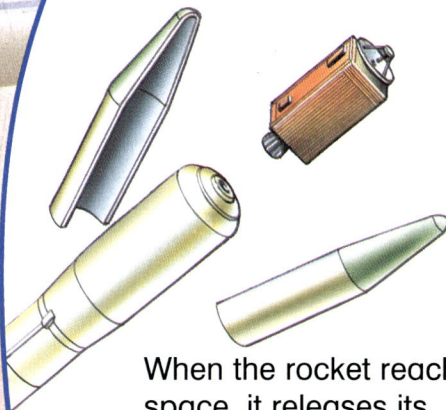

When the rocket reaches space, it releases its satellite **payload** into orbit.

M45

e esa

ariane

Helicopter

A helicopter takes off vertically from a very small space.

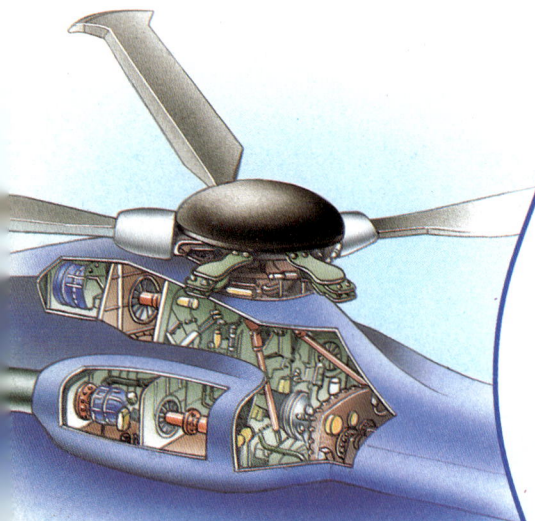

The main rotor is driven round by engines on either side of the helicopter.

The main rotor keeps the helicopter up in the air and also pushes it along.

A helicopter can take off and land straight up and down, so it doesn't need a runway. It can also hover in the air, and fly forwards and backwards, kept in the air by its spinning rotor blades. Helicopters are very useful for taking people into city centres fast. They are also used for rescuing people – from mountains and the sea.

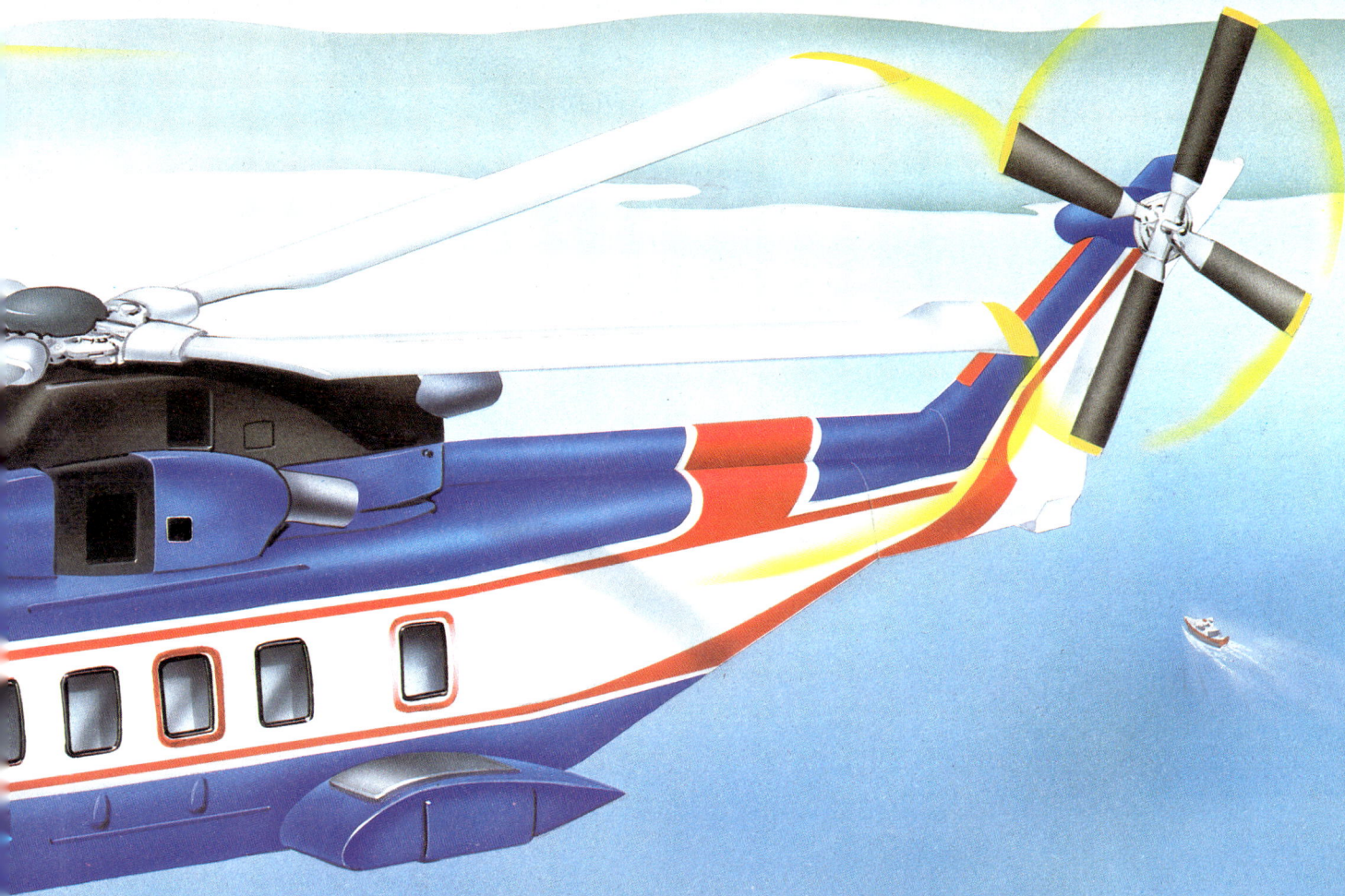

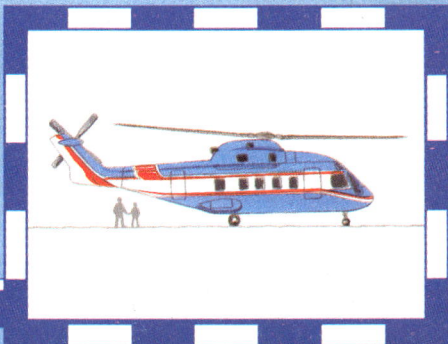

Hovercraft

A hovercraft is a special type of boat that skims over the surface of water. Underneath the hovercraft is a huge cushion of air. This keeps the hovercraft floating a few centimetres above the water. A huge **fan** pushes air into the cushion and a rubber 'skirt' stops the air escaping. Hovercraft are much faster than normal boats. Many hovercraft, like the one pictured here, carry both people and cars.

Cars drive on to the hovercraft on land. Then the hovercraft slides down into the water.

It is pushed along by propellers and steered by a large **rudder**.

The hovercraft skims back on to the smooth slipway at the end of its journey.

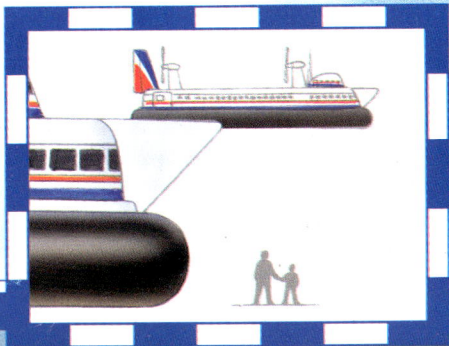

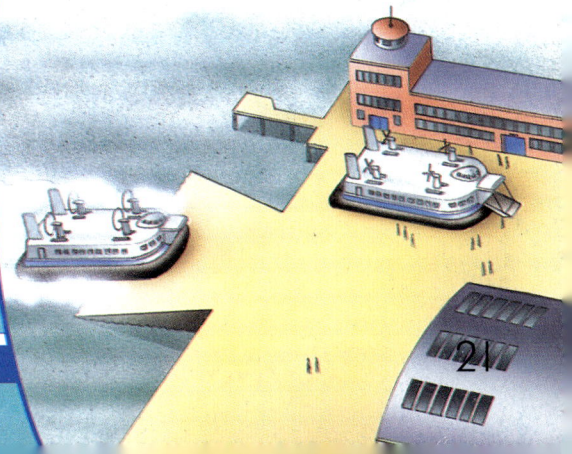

Fascinating Facts

Mobile Crane
The world's tallest crane can lift the weight of 30 family cars up to the top of a skyscraper.

Tunnel Boring Machine
Each TBM pulls a 200-metre long container train to carry the rocks and soil that have been dug out.

Car Crusher
Making steel from scrap metal uses approximately one quarter of the energy needed to make steel from natural resources.

Tree Processor
Computers are used to work out the best way to cut a log into pieces to make sure as much of the wood is used as possible.

Wind Turbine
Some wind turbines in North America are as tall as a 25-storey building.

Robot Arm
The word robot, comes from the Czech language, meaning worker.

Rocket
When a rocket takes off, at least nine tenths of its weight is made up of the fuel for its engines.

Helicopter
Helicopter plans were drawn over 500 years ago, but at the time, people did not understand how to build helicopters that would fly.

Hovercraft
The first hovercraft was invented by Sir Christopher Cockerell in Great Britain and built in 1959.

Glossary

Boom A long pole. One end of a boom is fixed to a machine and the other hangs in the air.

Diesel engine An engine which uses fuel called diesel oil. Many vehicles have diesel engines.

Fan A machine which pushes air from one place to another. It has spinning blades, like a propeller.

Generator A machine that makes electricity from a mechanical force, such as spinning turbine blades.

Hydraulic piston A machine which can give a push or pull. The piston is contained in a cylinder. Liquid is pumped in or out of the cylinder to make the piston move in or out.

Orbit A circular path an object takes around another object, such as the Earth orbiting the Sun.

Payload An object, such as a satellite, which is carried into space by a rocket.

Rudder A tall, flat piece of wood or metal that is attached to the back of a boat. The rudder is turned from side to side to steer the boat.

Satellite A scientific object made to orbit the Earth or a planet.

Spoil Rock and soil which are dug out of the ground when making a tunnel.

Weld To join two pieces of metal together by heating their edges up until they melt.

Index

Comparative sizes

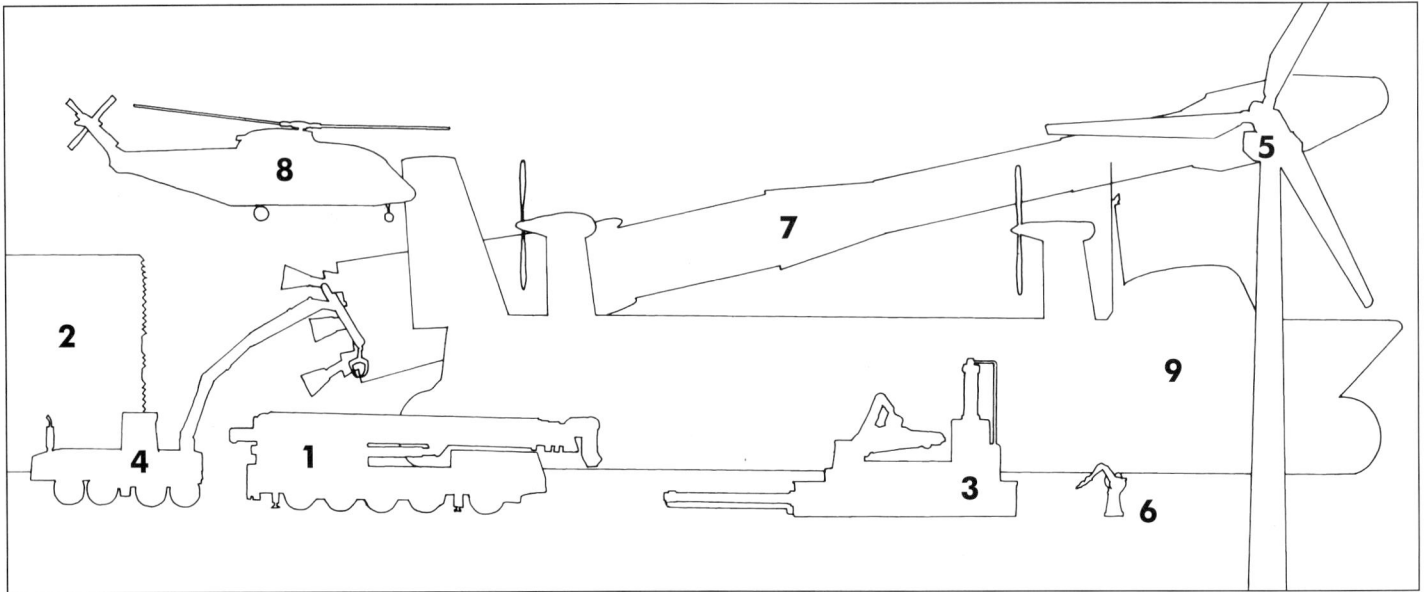

1 Mobile Crane

The boom of large mobile cranes can be extended to over 80 metres. This is more than the width of a football pitch.

2 Tunnel Boring Machine

The Channel Tunnel boring machine weighs 600 tonnes and moves forward at a speed of only eight metres per hour.

3 Car Crusher

Car crushers can crush a three-metre long car into a cube about a third of its size.

4 Tree Processor

When processing at full speed a tree processor can chop down and strip up to 60 trees an hour.

5 Wind Turbine

A modern wind turbine can produce enough electricity to provide power for 2,250 homes.

6 Robot Arm

Robot arms can do repetitive work for longer and much faster than a person can.

7 Rocket

When the *Ariane* rocket takes off it makes as much noise as 30 supersonic *Concorde* planes.

8 Helicopter

The rotor blades of this passenger helicopter are each about nine metres long.

9 Hovercraft

The largest passenger hovercraft in the world travels at a speed of 150 kilometres per hour.

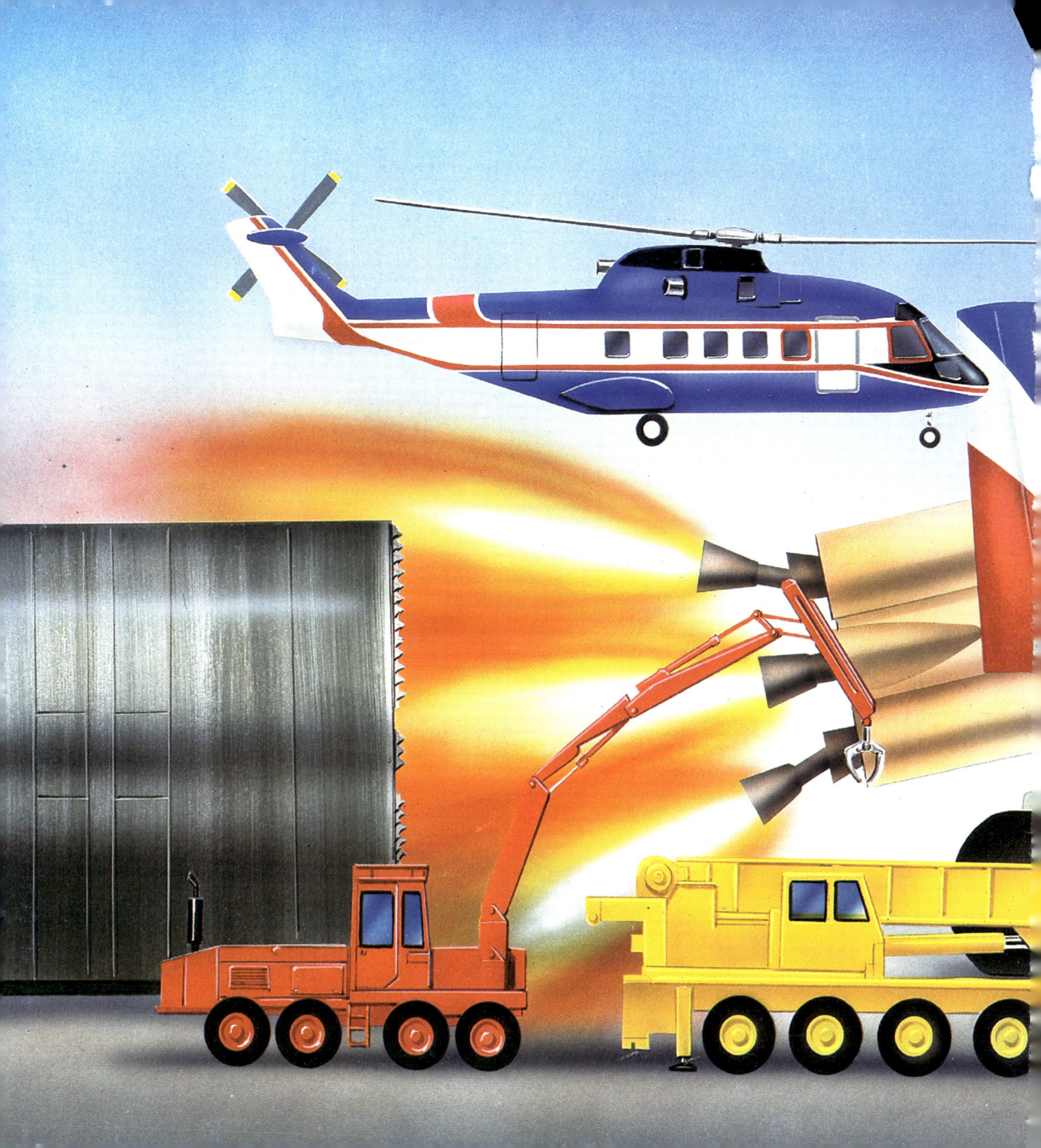